EUROPE CAN AFFORD TO WORK

EUROPE *Can* AFFORD TO WORK

Strategies for Growth and Employment in the European Community

FRANCIS CRIPPS & TERRY WARD
ARCA

SPOKESMAN
for
EUROPEAN LABOUR FORUM

The authors wish to thank other members of the Association for Applied Research in the European Community (ARCA), in particular, Ludo Cuyvers, Gerhard Leithäuser, Jacques Mazier, Pascal Petit and Enrico Wolleb, who provided valuable advice and material. None of these, however, bears any responsibility for the views expressed in the paper.

First published in Great Britain in 1993 by
Spokesman
Bertrand Russell House
Gamble Street
Nottingham, England
Tel. 0602 708318

British Library Cataloguing in Publication Data available on request from the British Library.

ISBN 0-85124-551-X
ISBN 0-85124-550-1 pbk

Printed by the Russell Press Ltd, Nottingham
(Tel. 0602 784505)

Contents

Foreword

When Bill Clinton was under sharpest attack from the Republicans about his personal life, about his supposed planned defection to the United Kingdom during the Vietnam war, and about practically everything else, his campaign manager stuck posters up on the wall with the legend "the economy, stupid". In other words, stick to economic issues, whatever mud the opposition throws at you, and whatever crops up, because it is on the credibility and coherence of the economic programme that you will be judged.

The leadership of the Socialist Group went to Stockholm in June 1992 to meet the four Scandinavian party leaders, and to talk with both Swedish government and opposition about enlargement.

During the discussions, the Group was stimulated by a speech and a paper from Allan Larsson, former Swedish finance minister, on the theme *Can Europe Afford not to Work*, which highlighted the costs of unemployment to Europe's economy, the difficulties facing full employment policies, and the overriding imperative to push growth and jobs as priority issues. Larsson's analysis demonstrates that more rapid economic growth is not always job-creating; a short-term random economic stimulus does not necessarily create lasting jobs.

Since our Stockholm meeting, unemployment has soared inexorably upwards; Europe's 10-year monetary stability has blown apart; the future of world trade negotiations is in jeopardy; and the Community countries are all in the grip of the deepest recession in 60 years.

For many months, Socialists have been calling for growth and employment issues to go to the top of the Community's agenda. The Parliamentary group and the Party of European Socialists launched their appeal before both the Birmingham and Edinburgh summits. Jacques Delors, from his corner, has been making the same plea. In the end, at Edinburgh, the first reaction came from the European Council, with a watered down growth and employment initiative, based principally on a new European Investment Bank facility. Certainly not enough. Certainly too limited in scope. Certainly not attacking the longer term causes of Europe's sluggish economic performance.

As our contribution to this debate, the Socialist Group organised, on 4 February 1993, a one-day special conference with Socialist party leaders, Socialist European and national parliamentarians, trade unions, representatives of industry, and financial and economic experts. To help focus our thoughts, we commissioned this paper from "ARCA", which Terry Ward introduced to the Conference.

The paper is not a blueprint. It is an analysis of the poor performance of the Community and the Member States over two decades, and is sober reading; inevitably, its prescription is, at this stage, skeletal.

By pooling our different national experiences and by seeking to spell out in far greater detail a Socialist alternative to failed Thatcherite economics, European Socialists have started a process.

The pursuit of this process will be at two levels, influencing the work of the Community institutions, particularly in the Parliament, in the Commission, and in those governments where we participate. It will also form the basis of our election programme for the 1994 European elections. The first point in our programme has to deal with the crisis facing the European economy. The credibility and relevance of that programme will be the test.

ARCA's contribution is a useful start.

Julian Priestley
Secretary General
Socialist Group
European Parliament

Introduction

The European Community in the 1990s faces severe problems of low growth, inadequate employment creation and high and rising unemployment, without the policy means of addressing these problems effectively.

During the present recession, which in 1992 spread right across Europe, the number of people out of work has risen virtually everywhere, in many places from levels which were already unacceptably high. Recovery is widely expected to be slow in coming and modest in scale.

On the European Commission's own prognosis (in its Communication to the Council before the Edinburgh Summit), even under favourable assumptions about the Community's capacity to create jobs, there is a high risk that the rate of unemployment will be at least 10-11% in 1996 — back to the peak level of the 1980s.

With slow growth and rising unemployment, social conditions are likely to worsen and standards of social welfare and justice, which have already come under pressure over the past two decades in many parts of Europe, will tend to decline.

Faced with this predicament, government leaders at the Edinburgh Summit in December made only a token gesture towards reviving the European economy. They failed to deliver the short-term measures urgently needed to stimulate demand in 1993 and pull the Community out of recession. Equally importantly, they failed to make any progress towards establishing a framework for policy coordination at the Community level, which is essential for sustaining growth and creating jobs in the longer-term.

Without such coordination, it will be difficult, if not impossible, for the Community to play its proper role in supporting growth in the global economy and to cooperate effectively with the US and Japan in managing economic and financial developments at the world level. It will also be less able to assist developing countries, especially in Central and Eastern Europe, North Africa and the Middle East, where economic growth is critical for long-term political stability and security in the region as a whole.

Indeed, instead of agreeing on closer cooperation, national governments and institutions have reiterated the importance of national sovereignty over economic policy and have made it clear that immediate national interests will continue to have precedence over Community-wide considerations.

Without a change in the attitude of a number of key decision-makers, it will be impossible to secure the agreement on the fundamental changes in the conduct of both monetary and fiscal policy required to achieve sustained recovery in the next few years, during Maastricht Stage 2. Indeed, pressure for budgetary consolidation on countries where public deficits and levels of debt exceed the Maastricht reference values threatens to slow recovery even further and make it more difficult to reduce unemployment.

This poses a major challenge for the left in Europe. Because of the severe constraints on national policy action, programmes for growth, employment creation and social justice require a Community-level platform for their effective implementation. If this does not seem credible, then electorates are less likely to give left parties their support. Instead, they will tend to turn to parties of the right, which lay stress on individual responsibility and do not pretend to have solutions for mass unemployment or widening disparities in income and employment opportunities.

In the face of the present political reality, the response of the left has to be to work over the long-term to establish a coherent framework for economic policy coordination at the Community level, with adequate democratic control over the decision-makers. In the short-term, the aim should be:

— to spell out the changes required in the conduct of monetary and fiscal policies so that they support rather than impede growth;

— to press for a strengthening of structural policies in order to boost development and job creation in those regions which are most in need, to emphasise the urgency of expanding investment in backward regions and in areas of industrial decline, and to stress the role of cities and local authorities as critical agents of development.

Above all, the left must put forward a credible perspective for change in the conduct of policy, to emphasise that sustaining adequate rates of growth and job creation, improving environmental infrastructure and achieving social goals have to be primary objectives of policy rather than residual aims to be tackled only once financial stability and low inflation have been secured.

Part One reviews political and economic problems confronting the Community, focusing particularly on the regional dimension of disparities in growth and employment creation across Europe. An appreciation of such disparities is a prerequisite for the formulation of an effective policy response.

Part Two outlines the main elements of a coherent strategy for addressing problems of slow economic growth and high unemployment in the context of the political situation which at present prevails.

The main aim is not to set out detailed policy proposals but to point the way towards a practical agenda for political action for the left in Europe in the coming years.

PART ONE

THE ECONOMIC AND POLITICAL BACKGROUND

CHAPTER 1

The Political Background

Further development of the Community, beyond simply obtaining agreement to Maastricht, is essential for the left in Europe. The policy objectives put forward by left parties, of sustained economic growth that creates jobs and generates the funds for social programmes while respecting environmental constraints, are only plausible in the context of close cooperation at the Community level. If Community-level action lacks credibility, then political support for the left is likely to recede.

In the 1980s, the Community was strengthened by new measures which provided an impetus and dynamic to the economy and which promised increased prosperity and more jobs in all regions. The most important was the resolution to achieve full integration of the internal market by 1st January 1993, to create the largest single market in terms of purchasing power in the world.

In parallel, however, there were major increases in Structural Funds to assist disadvantaged regions and increased emphasis on infrastructure links (Trans-European Networks), which together were designed to secure more balanced economic development across the Community, as well as the introduction of programmes aimed at coordinating technology development.

Parties on the left throughout Europe generally supported these developments and sought to protect the rights of workers and people generally by incorporating a social dimension through the Social Charter.

Widespread enthusiasm for the Single Market encouraged governments of Member States to negotiate the Maastricht Treaty, which defines plans for a staged transition to full monetary union and reinforces the Community's commitment to economic and social cohesion.

The Maastricht Treaty, however, has proved far more contentious than the Single Market. Despite the fact that, in terms of objectives, it strengthens the Community's commitment to balanced economic development, with increased regard for the environment and social cohesion, it has neither been presented nor generally perceived as providing the same kind of impetus to growth or the means of overcoming tangible problems — of lack of jobs and of social deprivation — which are of most concern to people in the Community.

The Treaty was heavily criticised by the European Parliament because it failed almost completely to address the problem of the lack of democratic accountability under existing institutional arrangements, let alone deliver any solution.

At present, the Community is effectively controlled by the Council of Ministers, a committee of national government leaders, in which policies have to be bargained in terms of domestic political pay-offs. In order to advance new initiatives the Commission is obliged to respond to the Council rather than to the European Parliament. At the same time, representation in the Council is confined to national groupings that participate in the national government, effectively excluding regions and interest groups which have different views and objectives.

By proposing increased powers for Community bodies without corresponding proposals to make these bodies more accountable, the Maastricht Treaty seems to distance policy-makers even further from the people and makes it even more difficult for the electoral process to have an influence on the decisions that are taken.

Public scepticism about the Maastricht proposals was reinforced by the disruption of the Exchange Rate Mechanism (ERM) in September 1992. The failure of Central Banks to resist financial market pressure and maintain exchange rates within agreed bands, together with the failure so far to come up with any concrete proposals for making any repetition of the experience less likely in the future, has made monetary unification seem a much more difficult and longer-term process.

Moreover, at the Edinburgh Summit in December 1992, governments of Member States refused to accept increases in the scale of the Community Budget that would have been necessary to give substance to the commitment to closer economic and social cohesion, which is a key aspect of the Treaty.

The expansion in the Community Budget agreed in Edinburgh will mean that, in relation to gross domestic product (GDP), it will be only marginally larger at the end of the decade than now, making it difficult to expand Community actions by very much. Although assistance to the poorer regions will increase markedly over this period through the expansion of the Structural Funds and the introduction of the new Cohesion Fund, financial transfers to these regions will still represent less than ½% of Community GDP in 1999 — enough to have a perceptible effect but nowhere near sufficient to fund the expenditure required to bring levels of economic and social infrastructure and support services and standards of education and training up to those in the rest of the Community.

At Edinburgh also, governments failed to respond to the issues of recession and high and rising unemployment, which are the principal concerns of most people in the Community. Despite the Commission's warning about the sharp deterioration in the short-term outlook and the need to take "decisive measures to address the situation", they contented themselves with announcing a small-scale package of investment measures spread over a number of years, which will have an imperceptible effect on economic activity. Nor did they take any significant action "aimed at reinforcing growth fundamentals and at encouraging job creation", which the Commission called for in response to the likelihood that unemployment would remain unacceptably high over the medium-term.

The Community seems to have reached an impasse over policy precisely at a time when action is urgently needed. Most national governments are in the position of trying to restore their credibility with their electorates either because they face an imminent election or because they have suffered major recent setbacks. No major government in Europe at present possesses the popular support to take the initiative in advocating a Community perspective for policy or a strengthening of central institutions. On the contrary, each is being forced by electoral considerations to give overriding priority to the defence of national interests.

Even if Maastricht Stage 2 arrangements are formally introduced as planned, on 1st January 1994, whatever their potential benefit, it seems unlikely at present that a common monetary policy will emerge or that the new arrangements will provide the basis for any new dynamic of growth and job creation. The United Kingdom's prime minister has stated that sterling will not rejoin the European Monetary System (EMS) in 1993, leaving it unclear how and when UK monetary policy could be reintegrated. More importantly, the Bundesbank has made it plain that, under Stage 2 arrangements, German monetary policy would continue exclusively to reflect national considerations.

At the same time, the proposals in the Treaty, if interpreted narrowly, concerning the need to pursue policies in Stage 2 that are aimed at reducing deficits and debt levels in those Member States where they exceed narrowly-specified limits, make low growth and inadequate job creation more likely.

Given the continuing fragmentation of monetary and fiscal policy and the differing problems facing individual Member States, the Council has not been able to face up to the recession and the large-scale destruction of jobs now in process. Hopes for economic recovery rest largely, as too often in the past, on an upturn in the United States, supported by the expansionary policies now being taken in Japan, and on an eventual improvement in European consumer and business confidence.

By failing to establish a joint framework for the conduct of monetary and fiscal policy, the Council has, moreover, made it more difficult for the Community to cooperate with the United States and Japan in regulating international financial markets, smoothing exchange rate fluctuations and supporting global economic growth. It is less able to respond to the opportunity for achieving more effective global economic management which the advent in the United States of a new — and potentially more sympathetic — President could provide.

Unemployment rates, 1991

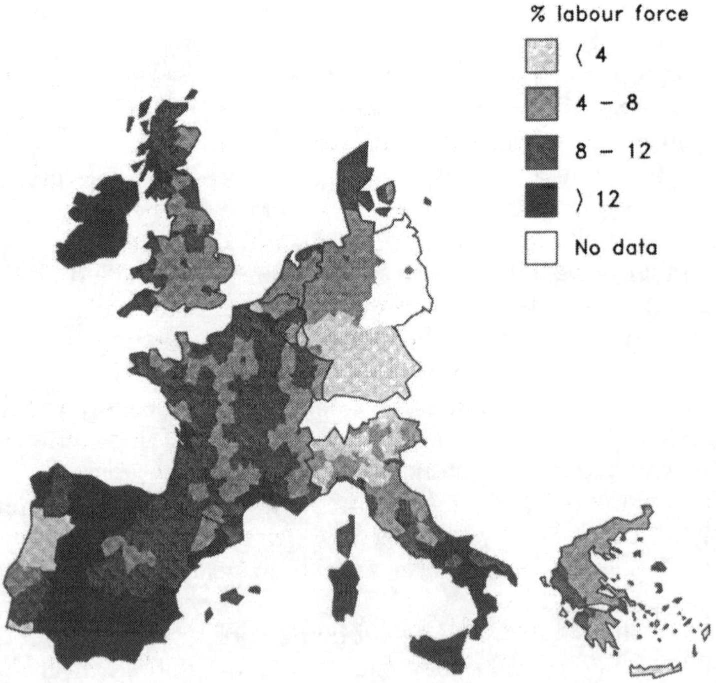

CHAPTER 2

The Community as a Slow-growth Area

Economic growth in the Community has been inadequate over the past 20 years, causing persistent problems of high unemployment, eroding government budgets and obstructing the development of backward regions. In 1974/5 and again in 1980/1, the interruption of economic growth in Europe could be blamed on oil crises. It is now, however, well over 10 years since the last oil crisis and it is by now clear that the loss of dynamic in the European economy has wider causes.

In the 1950s and 1960s, the Community was one of the most dynamic areas of the world economy with fast-growing trade and industry. Huge numbers of low-income farmers and agricultural workers as well as refugees from the East and immigrants from the South were absorbed into industrial and service jobs, while at the same time substantial shifts of employment from old, declining industries to new expanding ones took place relatively painlessly. Infrastructure and living conditions in backward regions improved dramatically.

Since 1973, the Community has been one of the least dynamic areas of the world economy. Economic growth has averaged only just over 2% over this period. No Member State has consistently succeeded in achieving a growth rate much above this, highlighting the high degree of interdependence between the national economies.

During this period, unemployment has risen in most countries to levels not experienced since the inter-war years as the rate of job creation has failed to keep pace with an expanding labour force.

Although some backward regions have continued to converge, the majority have remained blocked. Limited advances during phases of economic recovery have been wiped out as backward regions lost ground during phases of recession.

At the same time, many formerly prosperous regions have suffered deindustrialisation as traditional industries have contracted without being replaced by new growth sectors. Big increases in unemployment have been the result.

The continuing decline in agricultural employment in backward regions has barely been compensated by growth of service employment. Industrial sectors generally have ceased to provide significant numbers of new jobs as growth of output has been no higher — and in many cases much lower — than growth of productivity, stimulated by technological advance and increased competition in the Community and world markets.

Despite the low rate of economic growth, social cohesion has advanced steadily. Younger generations in all Member States aspire to similar lifestyles. Population growth has stabilised, family sizes have fallen everywhere and there has been a sustained increase in women's participation in the labour force throughout the Community.

Convergence of social patterns during past decades has brought considerable improvements in backward areas at a considerable cost to public budgets. Public provision of services and infrastructure has become increasingly unpopular in many parts of the Community, not only because of its high cost but also because it has continued to embody forms of paternalism — and sometimes corruption — which are not acceptable to modern generations.

Nevertheless the backlash against welfare programmes and programmes to assist less privileged areas has a high cost in regional and social terms.

As electorates everywhere demand reductions in tax burdens and direct value for money in public expenditure it is becoming increasingly difficult for governments to fund investment projects and/or transfers between countries and regions and even to redistribute income on a substantial scale between individuals.

In sum, the low rate of economic growth since the 1970s has created a vicious circle in which backward and deindustrialising regions experience high unemployment and have insufficient resources or opportunities to regenerate their economies.

More prosperous regions are suspicious of transfers in favour of low-income areas and reluctant to accept immigration. Yet stagnation of peripheral regions within and outside the Community deprives the wider European economy of a growth dynamic.

This has greatly increased the problems faced by countries in Central and Eastern Europe, struggling with ambitious programmes of political and economic reform and attempting massive restructuring of their economies, as well as by those in North Africa and the Middle East dependent on trade with the Community to support development. The stagnation of these surrounding regions in turn depresses markets for exports from the Community's more prosperous areas.

CHAPTER 3

The Regional Dimension of the Unemployment Problem

Low economic growth is reflected in enormous disparities across regions in unemployment and in the availability of resources to fund development. These disparities have long-run and deep-seated historical causes, cutting across businesses and social groups. In all cases, the key problem is inadequate rates of economic development and job creation rather than any failings on the part of the individuals who are unemployed. The disparities can only be effectively tackled by recognising the political and social nature of the underlying problems — inefficient public administration, inadequate levels of law and order, deficiencies in education and training and in the provision of social facilities, for example — as well as the economic factors involved.

Some of the most developed and prosperous regions — in Southern Germany and Northern Italy in particular — have succeeded in avoiding high unemployment completely because of their productive efficiency and capacity for generating income through both inter-regional and international trade. Most of the poorer, less developed regions predominantly in the South of the Community as well as older industrial areas in the North have, however, suffered substantial increases in unemployment since the mid-1970s.

In these regions, rates of unemployment are in many cases around 15-20% and in some local areas even higher (Graph 1). A high proportion of these unemployed, moreover, have been out of work for a prolonged period — at least a year and often much longer. In many areas of Southern Italy, Ireland and Spain, as well as in deindustrialising regions of Belgium, 60-70% or more of those recorded as unemployed have been without a job for a year or more.

Objective 1 and 2 Areas Eligible for Structural Funds

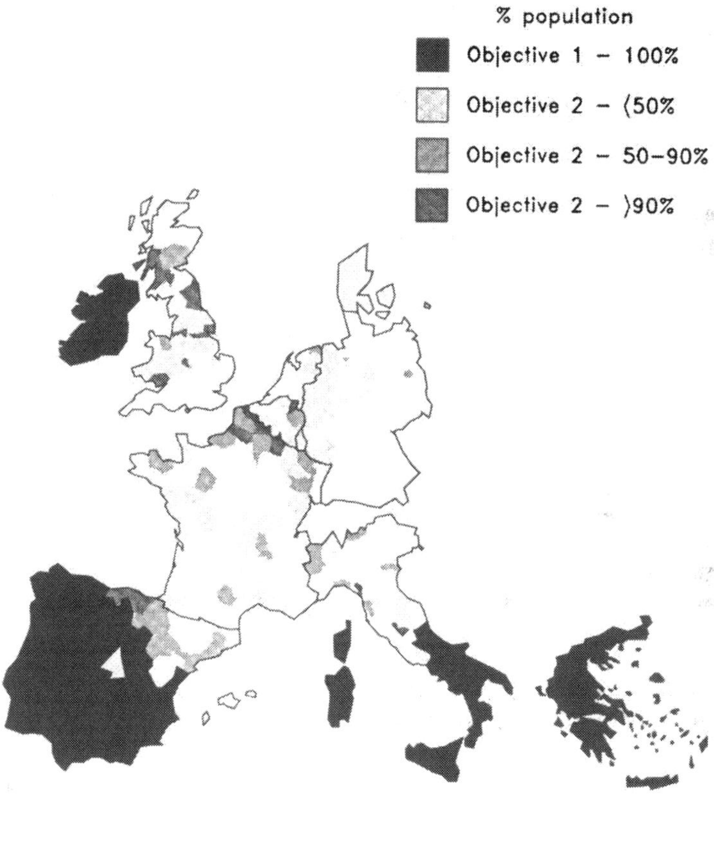

Objective 1 funds assist the less developed regions of the European Community.

Objective 2 funds support the regeneration of declining industrial areas.

1 Unemployment rates in Objective 1, Objective 2 and other regions in the Community, 1986 and 1991

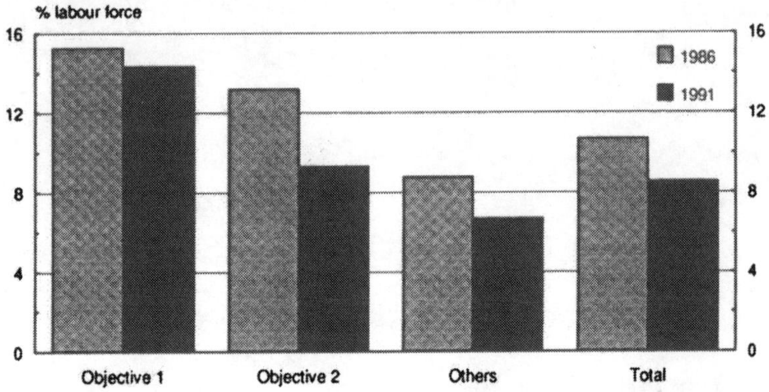

Substantial numbers of those out of work are young people under 25. Rates of unemployment for this age group now average over 32% in Objective 1 regions as a whole, with even higher rates in the worst affected areas (Graph 2). In these parts of the Community, the difficulties facing young people looking for a job, often for the first time, are acute and many have to resign themselves to a long spell of unemployment before finding work. In all Southern Member States, people under 25 make up well over a third of the

2 Youth unemployment rates in Objective 1, Objective 2 and other regions in the Community, 1986 and 1991

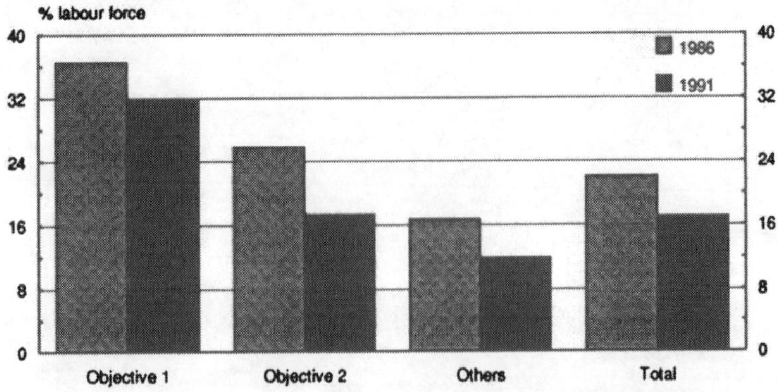

Unemployment rates of young people (<25), 1991

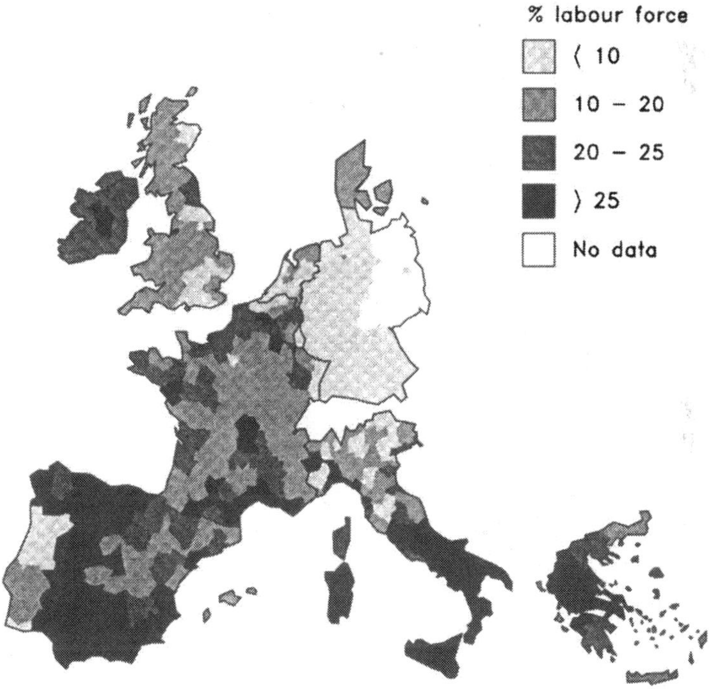

long-term unemployed, and in Greece and Italy well over 40%.

In the more industrialised Northern parts of the Community, long-term unemployment is more a problem of older age groups, particularly those losing their job in middle age who find it difficult to find alternative work because employers prefer to take on younger recruits, and because not enough new jobs are being created to replace those lost.

In most of the high unemployment regions, especially in the South, the true scale of the problem is disguised by people — especially women — being deterred by the acute shortage of work from entering the labour market at all. Recorded rates of inactivity in these regions tend to be much higher than elsewhere, concealing large numbers of people who are effectively unemployed even if they are not counted in the official figures. In addition, many of those who are employed work in low-paid and insecure jobs under barely tolerable conditions.

On reasonable assumptions (comparing inactivity rates with those in the most economically and socially developed areas), concealed unemployment can be put at around double the numbers actually recorded as unemployed over large areas of the Community. In the less developed regions as a whole, concealed unemployment is probably over 15% of people of

3 Estimates of concealed unemployment in Objective 1, Objective 2 and other regions in the Community, 1986 and 1991

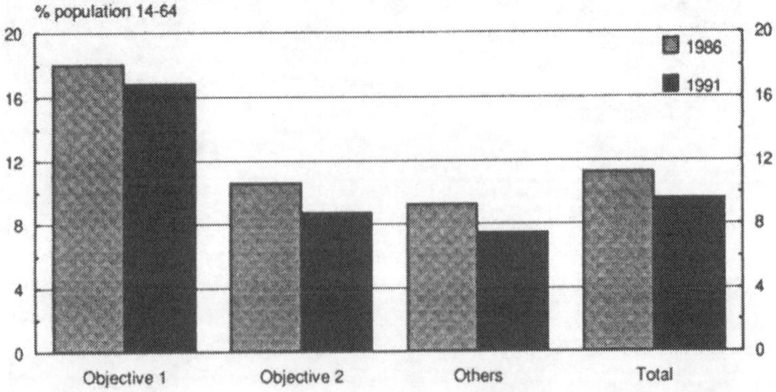

Estimates of concealed unemployment rates in the Community, 1991

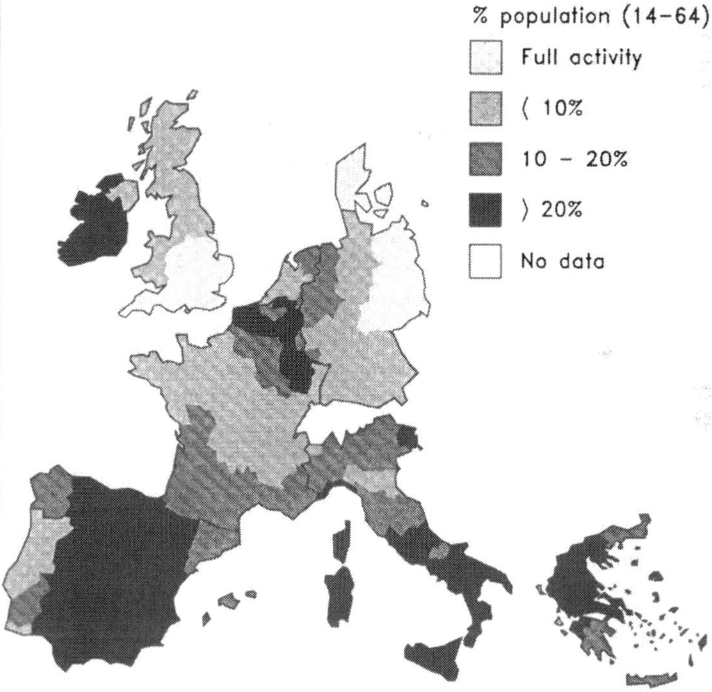

working age (Graph 3), implying that over 25% of people of working age are probably either openly unemployed or forced to be inactive because of job shortages, and in parts of Southern Italy and Spain, over a third.

This gives an indication of the true scale of the problem which needs to be confronted. The problem, moreover, is made worse by the fact that, despite substantial falls recently in the birth rate in Southern European countries, the population of working age in the less developed parts of the Community is set to go on increasing significantly over the next 10 years — and indeed longer — whereas in many of the more prosperous regions it is likely to grow very slowly or to decline. The rate of job creation which is required in coming years to have any substantial impact on levels of unemployment — concealed as well as open — in less developed regions is, therefore, considerable.

CHAPTER 4

Growth and Regional Employment

Higher sustained growth in the Community is a necessary condition for narrowing regional disparities in job creation and unemployment. On past evidence, both less developed and deindustrialising regions are especially affected by cyclical fluctuations in the growth of the Community economy. Periods of high growth tend to be periods of convergence in income per head and employment — periods of low growth or recession are periods of divergence. This is a reflection partly of the structure of activity in these regions, partly of their peripheral location and their reliance on financial inflows from the rest of the Community.

Experience in the second half of the 1980s, when the Community achieved a higher rate of employment growth than at any time since the 1950s, is instructive in illustrating both what future recovery might achieve and the limitations of growth *per se* in securing employment objectives. (At the country level, there was some tendency over this period for employment to rise by more in those countries where GDP growth was highest, and no country with low growth managed to increase employment significantly — with the partial exception of the Netherlands where there was a major rise in part-time working — Graph 4.)

In the first half of the 1980s, output in the Community grew only slowly and unemployment rose in most places, but especially in the areas of industrial decline — Objective 2 regions — where jobs losses in industry were substantial and unemployment went up significantly. In the second half of the 1980s, however, when recovery occurred, employment increased significantly faster in the deindustrialising regions taken together than elsewhere in the Community, with growth

4 GDP growth and employment change 1985-1990

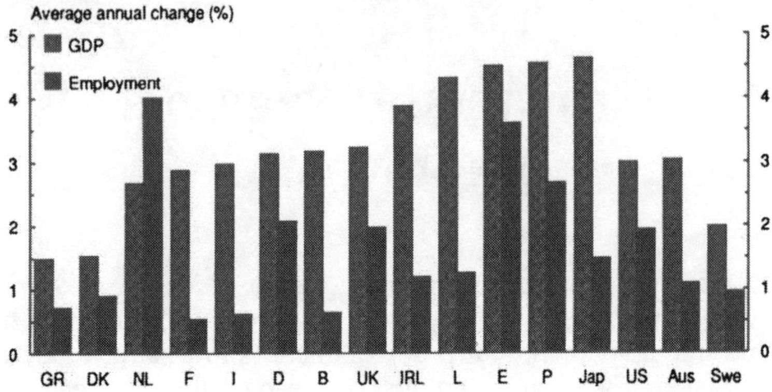

generating significant job creation in services (Graph 5). As a result, unemployment fell by much more than in other regions. The reduction, however, was not universal. In some regions of France unemployment went up rather than down.

In less developed Objective 1 regions, the picture is more complicated. In aggregate, these regions experienced an increase in jobs in both industry and services similar in percentage terms to the increase in Objective 2 regions, and higher than the more developed, prosperous parts of the Community. But large-scale job losses in agriculture, which remains an important occupation in these regions, meant that

5 Change in employment by sector in Objective 1, Objective 2 and other regions, 1986-1990

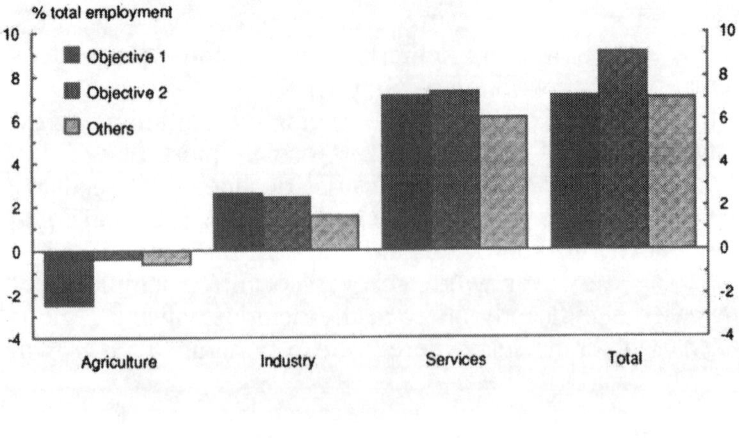

Changes in unemployment rates, 1986-1990

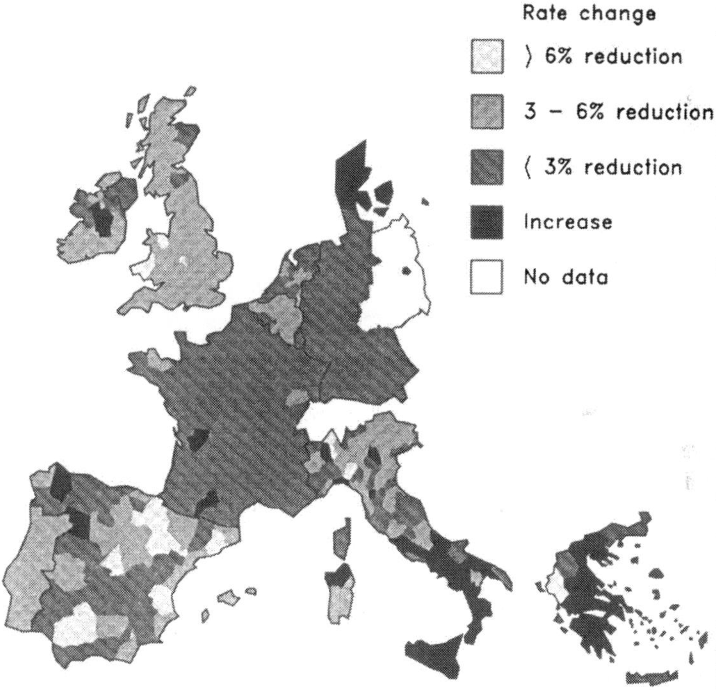

in total employment rose by much less than in Objective 2 regions, and by no more than in the most prosperous regions.

There were, however, marked differences in experience between different areas, with regions in Spain and Portugal generally recording above average growth of employment, those in Southern Italy, Greece and Ireland, below average. As a result, unemployment in the latter regions either went up or fell by less than elsewhere, while in many parts of Spain and Portugal the unemployment rate came down by more than in prosperous regions. In aggregate, partly because of continued labour force growth, there was very little reduction in total unemployment in Objective 1 regions during the period of recovery.

Several lessons can be drawn from this experience. First, most regions in need of employment creation are likely to benefit from renewed growth in the Community, but it is not inevitable that all will. Secondly, because of the high proportion of employment that remains in agriculture in the less developed regions, jobs have to be created there at a much higher rate in industry and services than elsewhere, just to provide work for those leaving the land. Thirdly, because of higher prospective labour force growth — given both continuing growth of working-age population and increasing participation on the part of women — the overall growth of employment in these regions has to be especially high to prevent unemployment from increasing.

There are two further lessons. First, high employment growth tends to mean far more job opportunities for young people and, therefore, the rate of unemployment for the under 25 age group is likely to come down by more than for older people, just as it tends to rise more in recession. This makes it easier to tackle the problem of youth unemployment.

Secondly, employment growth will not necessarily mean any relative reduction in long-term unemployment. The average proportion unemployed for a year or more in the Community was only slightly lower in 1990 than in 1985. In Italy, Greece and Ireland, it was higher. This means that labour market action directed specifically at helping the long-term unemployed is essential to avoid significant numbers of people being deprived of work more or less permanently.

Changes in the unemployment rates of young people, 1986-1990

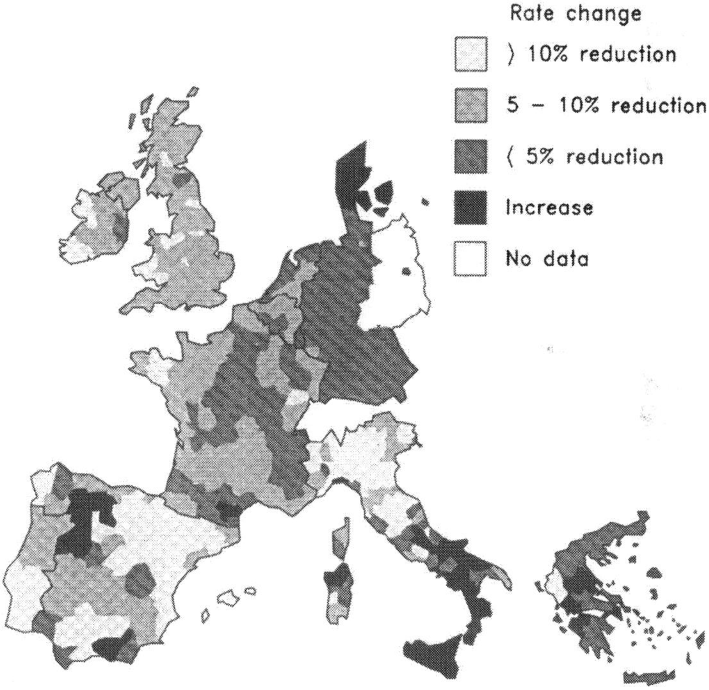

CHAPTER 5

Obstacles to Expansionary Economic Policies

The highly integrated nature of the Community economies and their close trading and financial links with the rest of the world are potential sources of economic strength. However, given the present fragmented state of policy-making in the Community, they can contribute to low growth and inhibit the adoption of more expansionary policies. At the same time, regional divisions profoundly condition politics at the national and European level. The more prosperous countries and regions, particularly in a context of low growth, tend to be intent on protecting their own position, and unwilling to transfer income to backward or depressed areas.

This division is reflected in differences in policy objectives, especially in the weight given to price stability as opposed to growth and employment creation. Until the balance of power in the Community shifts away from those areas giving overriding priority to stability — and therefore to low levels of credit creation and borrowing — any significant reorientation of policy will remain problematic.

Since the oil price crises of 1973/4 and 1979/80 emphasis on cautious monetary policies has generally held sway. The close trading and financial links between the Community and other parts of the world have meant that the Community economy has been greatly affected by fluctuations in activity elsewhere. Moreover, because of the highly integrated nature of the European economy, reinforced by the Single Market, a downturn or upturn in any one member country has quickly spread to other parts.

The coincident movement over recent years in real asset values in major parts of the world — which are both a cause and reflection of fluctuations in spending and, therefore,

6 Inflation-adjusted stock market prices, US, UK, Japan, Germany and France, 1966-1991

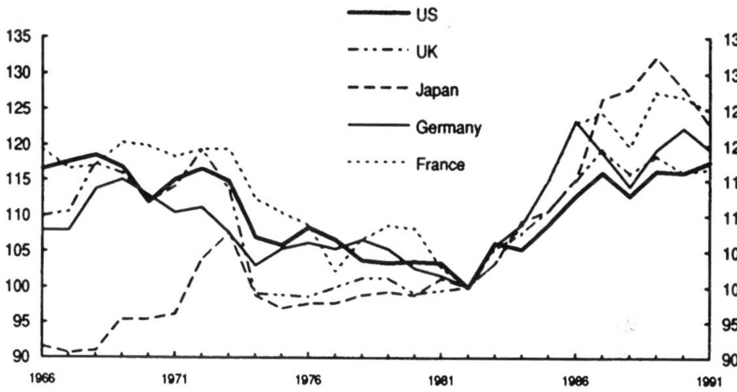

economic activity — demonstrates the close links that exist between countries and the high degree of economic interdependence which results (illustrated in Graphs 6 and 7, which show real share prices and residential property prices).

Faced with a downturn in external demand, governments in the Community have often responded by reducing rather than expanding internal demand, cutting public expenditure and/or increasing taxes in an attempt to contain increases in public deficits. By so doing, they have reinforced the

7 Inflation-adjusted property prices (residential), US, Japan and the UK, 1982-1991

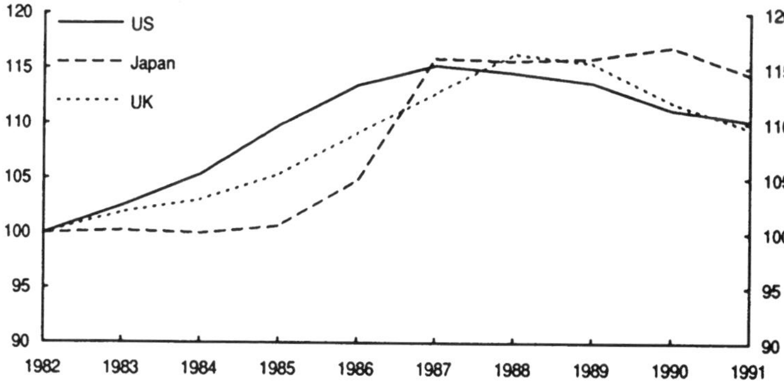

recessionary impetus not only in their own economies but also elsewhere.

Such perverse action reflects a shift in the trade-off between internal and external policy considerations, which has been reinforced by integration of trade and capital markets without parallel monetary unification. Action to stimulate internal demand is now more likely to benefit producers elsewhere than domestic businesses, and creates disproportionate financial problems for the country that provides the stimulus. Extreme caution in national fiscal and monetary policies has been encouraged by pressure from the international financial market, which has become of increasing influence as the liquidity of foreign exchange transactions — and, therefore, the speed at which commitments can be converted from one currency to another — has grown.

Rather than run the risk of provoking capital outflows, a possibly uncontrollable fall in their exchange rate, increased inflation and a financial crisis, governments have in general opted to follow 'strong money' policies.

The experience of individual countries — the UK in the mid-1970s and of France in the early 1980s, for instance — which attempted to break out of recession by sustaining internal demand and which very soon encountered financial crisis, provides a powerful lesson of the dangers of unilateral attempts to resist international recession.

Initial steps towards monetary union, in particular, the commitment to maintaining fixed exchange rates for prolonged periods under the ERM, and the abolition of exchange controls, have tightened the constraint on unilateral pursuit of more expansionary policies by individual Member States.

The result is that Community countries collectively have helped spread and intensify recession by the policy action — or lack of it — which they have taken in the past, and have contributed almost nothing to stimulating recovery at the global level. Instead, they have been content to wait for other regions of the world to take the lead in expanding demand.

Although the size of its market gives the Community the potential to play a major role in managing world economic activity — which would be an immense benefit not only to other countries, especially those in neighbouring regions to the East and South, but to the Community itself — this potential will remain unexploited so long as economic policy continues to be uncoordinated, and so long as the priority in the more prosperous and powerful regions of the Community remains one of narrow short-term self-interest.

The recent downturn in the German economy, the substantial fall in industrial production experienced over the past year, and the rapid rise in unemployment may, from this perspective, be a favourable development insofar as these events may cause some reconsideration of policy objectives and priorities in the most prosperous parts of the Community.

It may, in particular, lead to a reassessment of the risk to inflation associated with the adoption of more expansionary policies, a risk which, in practice, in a period of deep recession, with high unemployment, substantial underutilised resources and massive excess capacity, is likely to be low. (In the 1980s, faster growth in most countries was not accompanied by any significant rise in inflation.) More pertinently, it may also lead to a comparison of this risk with the misery created by unemployment and lack of opportunity and the near-certainty of increasing social — and political — unrest.

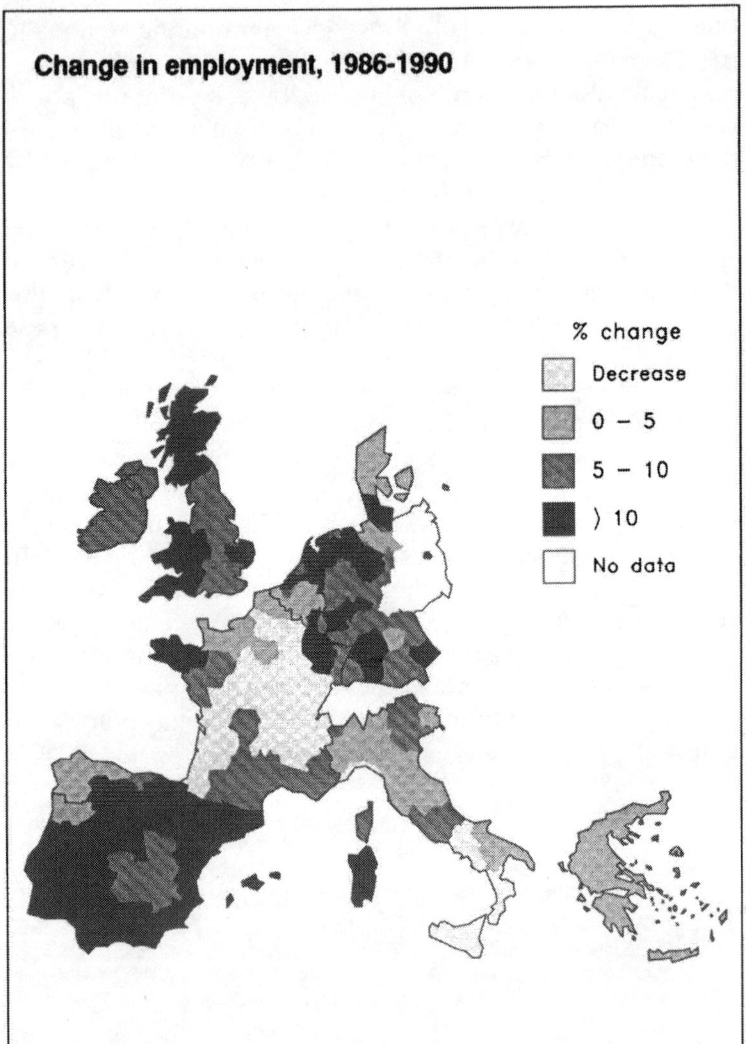
Change in employment, 1986-1990
% change
Decrease
0 – 5
5 – 10
⟩ 10
No data

PART TWO

KEY ELEMENTS OF A STRATEGY FOR GROWTH AND EMPLOYMENT

CHAPTER 6

The Need for Policy Action at the Community and Local Level

An effective response by the left to slow growth and rising unemployment in the Community needs to emphasise the importance of policy action at two levels:

— at the Community level to provide the necessary framework for accelerated economic development both within Western Europe and in neighbouring regions in Central and Eastern Europe, Africa and the Middle East;

— at the regional, local and city level, where authorities have to deal directly with the social consequences of low growth and inadequate employment creation, and must be the prime movers in any modern, decentralised pattern of development.

A left programme for sustained recovery and increased convergence of levels of income and employment must, therefore, incorporate, on the one hand, a demand for a strengthening of Community institutions so that they become capable of managing economic policy, and of providing a coordinated monetary framework, and, on the other, an increased emphasis on resource transfers and a legislative framework to support investment and development at the regional and city level.

The aim should be to sustain a rate of economic growth in the Community as a whole of 3-4%, instead of the rate of only just over 2% achieved over the past 20 years, with higher rates in less developed regions and areas of industrial decline, and lower rates in the more prosperous regions where growth *per se* is not an overriding priority.

A rate significantly lower than this is likely to make it impossible in practice to create sufficient job opportunities to reduce unemployment to acceptable levels within the next two decades. Nor would a lower growth rate in Western

Europe provide a viable context for reform and restructuring in Central and Eastern Europe, North Africa and the Middle East.

A lower growth rate — and the inequalities associated with low growth — will also make it difficult to fund social programmes within the Community and action to protect and improve the environment, activities that are widely supported in their own right, and are an important potential source of employment.

CHAPTER 7

A Framework for Monetary Policy

Monetary stability is critical as a foundation for sustained investment and growth of private and public sector spending. The monetary system as it now exists, however, with only loose cooperation between central banks, has failed to deliver the required stability. Moreover, by giving rise to high real interest rates without removing uncertainty about future exchange rates, it has served to depress growth in the Community. The aim should be to ensure that, in a context of low growth and high unemployment, monetary policy helps governments to finance deficits caused by recession, and funds investment in infrastructure and new business development in support of recovery.

To secure monetary stability and to facilitate credit expansion requires close coordination in the operation of monetary policy. However, although countries in the Community have problems in common, there is no clear tendency, partly because of differing priorities, towards increased cooperation in this area. These differences in priorities reflect the substantial disparities in economic performance that still exist between Member States, and which stand to widen the longer recession goes on. So long as they persist, they represent a major obstacle to monetary unification. Recent upheavals in exchange markets make it clear that ECU parities for national currencies cannot be enforced arbitrarily in the face of divergent economic conditions in Member States. Businesses and financial investors recognize that differences in inflation rates, public debt, unemployment and trade balances will, sooner or later, have to be compensated by realignment of exchange rates. The significant divergence in real exchange rates of major

8 Variation in real exchange rates for the five largest Member States, 1970-1991

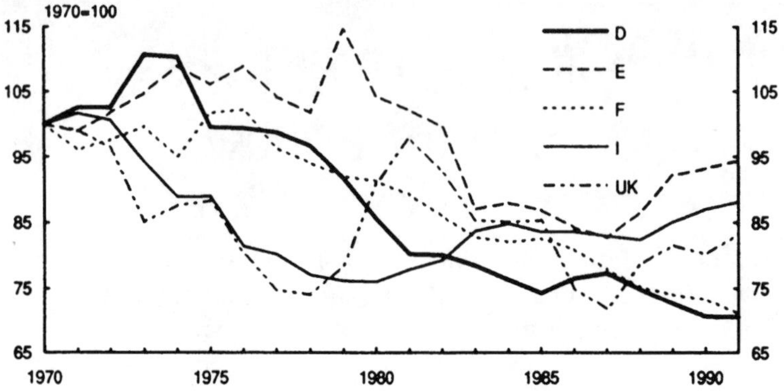

European currencies in the latter part of the 1980s and early 1990s (Graph 8), which resulted from maintaining nominal rates while rates of inflation and productivity performance differed, could not feasibly have continued for very much longer.

The implication is that full monetary union, with a single currency and, therefore, permanently fixed exchange rates, will only become feasible progressively as and when a greater degree of economic convergence — real as well as nominal — is achieved.

The present situation is difficult since the Single Market makes fluctuations in exchange rates and differences in costs of borrowing in different parts of the Community very important problems for business, while remaining differences in economic structure and national institutions prevent monetary unification.

Ideally, Maastricht Stage 2 should provide a framework for much closer coordination of national monetary policies in order to provide financial stability, and prevent the kind of upheaval that occurred in September 1992. Despite reservations expressed by the Bundesbank and some national governments, risks to business could be much reduced through joint management of national currencies, respecting differences in national situations according to systematic criteria.

The formula for monetary policies in Europe must be flexibility, delivering effective stability of financial conditions, with a bias towards convergence.

For example, there is an inevitable presumption that divergences in real (inflation-adjusted) exchange rates and real interest rates have to be kept within bounds by periodic adjustments of nominal rates. There are also lesser, but not entirely unreasonable, presumptions that countries with weak trade balances may require lower real interest rates and exchange rates for transitional periods, provided that lower real exchange rates do not feed back too strongly into inflation. Equally, countries with high inflation but relatively strong trade balances may benefit from higher real exchange rates exerting pressure in favour of price stability.

During the 1980s, there was considerable emphasis on management of monetary policy according to quantitative targets for monetary aggregates, at the cost of rather wide fluctuations in interest rates in many Member States (Graph 9, which shows not only large fluctuations in real interest rates in some countries but also a marked tendency for rates within the Community to move together). Disillusion with the results of 'monetarist' experiments has resulted in a more pragmatic attitude which ought to permit central banks to take a wider range of indicators into account. Doctrinal emphasis on

9 Real short-term interest rates in the five largest Member States and the Community, 1970-1991

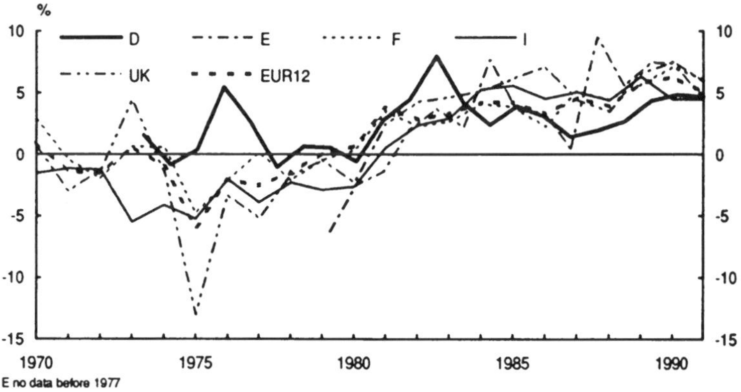

monetary convergence carries risks similar to those implied by the former emphasis on monetary aggregates.

Provided that the need for flexibility is recognized, it should be possible for central banks, working closely together, to ensure reasonable stability of real exchange rates and real interest rates within the Maastricht Stage 2 framework, so long as the opportunity for coordinated monetary management that this provides is properly exploited.

Such cooperation is of major importance in supporting sustained recovery across the Community. While the action taken by the UK government to disengage from the ERM and allow its exchange rate to depreciate may help stimulate domestic growth, it is an illusion to imagine that a freely floating rate represents a viable long-term strategy for the United Kingdom, still less an example to be followed by other Member States.

Although short-term policy constraints may be weaker for a country with a freely floating exchange rate, uncertainty is substantially increased, and businesses forced to gamble on week-to-week currency movements will have greater difficulty in making long-term commitments of investment and production.

The United Kingdom government, in September 1992, was in a position where it had no option but to devalue, either inside or outside the ERM. It was also in a position where, with low inflation, the risk of increased price increases was less intimidating than the consequences of continuing slump and high and rising unemployment. As time goes on, the balance of priorities is likely to change, and the need to ensure exchange rate stability will again become important. In practice, the UK example may demonstrate the defects of the current EMS. But it can also be interpreted as demonstrating the need to strengthen monetary cooperation and to operate the ERM in a more flexible manner, so that governments are not driven to take unilateral action, which works against Community interests and, ultimately, their own.

CHAPTER 8

A Framework for Fiscal Policy

The anti-growth bias of monetary policy has been compounded by a bias in attitudes to public expenditure and deficit-financing in particular, which has caused governments to seek to limit spending and reduce borrowing even where increases were the direct result of recession and reduced private investment. In future, the aim should be to establish a framework for stable management of public expenditure and taxation over the long term, to prevent policy reinforcing fluctuations in economic activity rather than smoothing them.

The slowdown in economic growth of the Community since the mid-1970s has created long-term fiscal problems in all Member States. Revenue shortfalls in each cyclical recession have tended to push up the ratio of public debt to GDP, although in some countries this has been offset by privatisation (notably in the UK). In the Community as a whole the ratio of public debt to GDP has risen from 50% in the early 1980s to over 60% in 1992. In some member countries (Belgium, Italy, Ireland and Greece) public debt has risen to 100% or more of annual GDP.

At the same time, governments have in general tried to contain increases in budget deficits caused by slow growth. Although real interest rates have risen in the recent past to unprecedented levels, there is no evidence that these have been required to fund excessive budget deficits or, indeed, that reducing deficits is necessary to bring interest rates down. In fact, real interest rates were lower in the first half of the 1980s than since then, despite budget deficits being higher (Graph 10). Contrary to the widespread view that still dominates policy-making, the present high interest rates across the Community have little to do with levels of

10 Net borrowing of general government and real short-term interest rates in the Community, 1981-1991

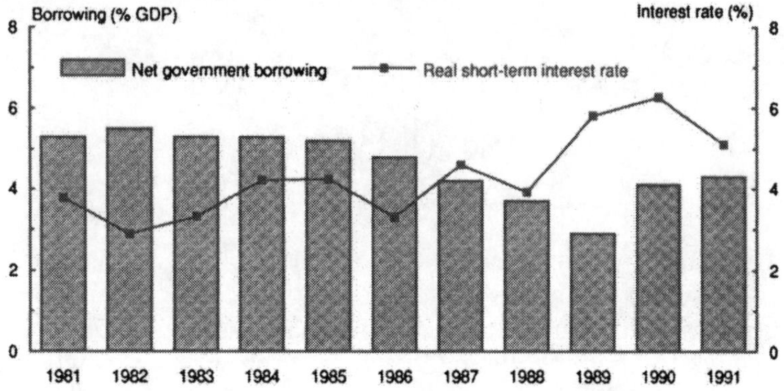

government borrowing. Instead, they reflect the prevailing desire to limit credit creation, restrain demand, maintain a strong exchange rate, and keep down inflation.

In the present recession, the reduction in revenue resulting from the erosion of the tax base, and the increased expenditure caused by higher unemployment and lower activity, are likely to be responsible for public deficits rising across the Community as a whole by an estimated 3-4% of GDP — equivalent to ECU 225-300 billion — in 1993.

These high levels of public debt, and the tendency towards large budget deficits that has caused them, increase the difficulties of managing monetary policy in the Community and of moving towards monetary union. The reaction in the Maastricht Treaty, if narrowly interpreted, is to impose ceilings on the scale of both debt and public deficits in relation to GDP, to monitor policy in the light of these levels, and to establish an eventual procedure for compelling Member States to eliminate excessive levels.

What needs to be emphasised are the repercussions of the required reductions in public expenditure, and/or increases in taxes, on economic activity both in the country attempting to reduce its deficit and in the rest of the Community. Without Member States with levels of public debt and budget deficits below the ceilings taking compensating expansionary action, there is a danger that the overall growth of demand in the

Community will tend to be depressed, with consequent effects on output and employment.

To avoid curbing economic growth in this way, there are essentially three options.

The first is to abandon the budgetary convergence criteria in Maastricht entirely, and allow each Member State to determine the level of deficit and debt that it considers appropriate, given its need for public services and investment in infrastructure.

The second is to establish a financial instrument at the Community level, funded by the issue of Community debt and, therefore, not counting as a component of public debt of individual Member States, to assist countries that are required to reduce debt levels.

The third option, which could be adopted alongside the second, is to interpret the criteria as medium-term benchmarks and, therefore, not require governments to take action likely to exacerbate the downturn in activity during periods of recession, such as the present time. Such an interpretation is consistent with the Treaty provision establishing a mechanism for resolving questions about appropriate budgetary action in particular circumstances (in consultation with the European Parliament).

The first option seems unrealistic. It would place reliance entirely on financial market forces to restrain excessive borrowing, would carry the risk, if these were not sufficiently powerful, of undermining monetary management, and would confirm fears in the Bundesbank and elsewhere about moves towards monetary unification being accompanied by a relaxation of discipline on spend-thrift governments and a flow of investable funds in their direction.

The second option has much to commend it. Debt creation at the Community level does not involve the same 'crowding out' objections levelled against increases in public debt at the national level and, since it has no implications for exchange rates between Community currencies, there is no reason why it should lead to any rise in interest rates. Moreover, a significant facility — an amount equivalent to, say, ½% of Community GDP — could be created at comparatively modest cost in terms of interest payments.

At least 8 of the 12 Member States now have public deficits in excess of the Maastricht guideline (3% of GDP), and 6 have public debt well in excess of the Maastricht limit (60% of GDP). In most cases, the size of public deficits and public debt is related to needs for expenditure on education, social services and infrastructure that exceed the national resources. In the absence of a Community debt instrument to assist debt reductions in Member States, it is unrealistic to expect the Maastricht limits to be achieved in the present decade, and it is liable to be highly damaging to economic and social cohesion if the Member States concerned made a serious attempt to do so. (The Cohesion Fund established at Edinburgh for essentially the same purpose — though confined to the poorer countries — is far too small, at a mere ECU 15 billion spread over 7 years, to ease the difficulties other than marginally.)

Debt financing at the Community level could also counteract the contractionary bias imparted to national policies by the existing multi-currency monetary system. The Community should be able to make good revenue shortfalls and support public authorities at national and local level through cyclical downturns by funding part of its own Budget and rebating contributions from Member States.

The major obstacle to the creation of such a facility is political rather than economic. Governments have made it plain that they are unwilling at present to contemplate any substantial expansion of borrowing facilities at the Community level, a reluctance which seems to stem from the prevailing attitude towards public sector borrowing *per se* rather than the Community-level dimension of the proposal.

The third option of planning budgetary policy over the medium-term seems, at present, to offer the most promising basis for agreement, and is consistent with orthodox economic thinking. During periods of recession, governments ought to experience little difficulty in funding the increased deficit that results from a downturn in economic activity and which, in practice, is a reflection of a reduction in private expenditure and a loss of confidence in private assets. Indeed, by creating more debt they will in effect be compensating for the reduction in private sector debt that is likely to occur as the willingness of business to invest declines and, therefore, 'crowding in' rather than 'crowding out' investment.

Moreover, by establishing a stable medium-term path for public expenditure and tax rates, such an approach could make a major contribution to countering cyclical fluctuations in economic activity. It would allow public expenditure to expand, and the revenue collected by government to decline, as private sector activity fell, so helping to offset this decline, while having a restraining effect if growth was excessive.

The evidence from a number of countries is that deliberate policy action taken by governments to stabilise activity is just as likely to increase fluctuations as to reduce them, because of often lengthy time lags between action being seen to be required and its impact on the economy. Maintaining a smooth growth path for public expenditure, and avoiding sudden changes in tax rates, may, therefore, be in general the most effective stabilisation policy that governments can follow.

It is essential, however, that all governments within the Community agree on such an approach, and support those whose deficits are increased by recession, in order to provide protection against financial market pressure.

CHAPTER 9

Problems of Funding Public Expenditure

The bias against public debt, together with the failure of the monetary system to protect national currencies against financial market pressure, has not only prevented governments from sustaining spending during recession; it has thereby contributed to low growth and deprived less developed and deindustrialising regions of finance for public services, income support and investment, while making the cost of borrowing prohibitively expensive. This bias against public spending, and against raising the revenue from both taxes and borrowing to finance it, needs to be corrected if balanced development across the Community is to be supported.

During earlier decades, tax revenues tended to rise as a share of GDP, providing rapid growth in resources for public expenditure. The reluctance of taxpayers to continue to support large public budgets has several causes. In a climate of recession or slow economic growth people are less willing to give up control over their income unless they know precisely how they personally will benefit. When public services come under financial pressure, standards tend to suffer and the confidence of those employed in the public sector is eroded.

In a context of increased competition, reinforced by the Single Market, and high unemployment caused by slow growth, people also fear that high taxes and social contributions will cost jobs. Reducing the tax burden and the cost of employment below levels in other countries becomes a means of gaining competitive advantage and of creating jobs, even though by damaging public services and infrastructure such a policy is liable, over the longer term, to erode any advantage gained in the short term.

During the past decade there has been little or no convergence of the fiscal systems of Member States. The share of GDP taken by government revenue varies between around 50% in France and the Netherlands to around 35% in Spain and the UK, while the structure of taxation shows equally substantial differences. In particular, the level of social contributions and, therefore, the non-wage element of labour costs which employers face is 2-3 times higher in France, Italy and Belgium than in Denmark or the UK. Rates of taxes on business profits also vary markedly between countries.

The low level of the overall burden of taxation in the UK and Spain help to keep costs of employment down in these countries, and may help attract businesses for which low labour costs are a major competitive factor. Conversely, high revenue shares in France and the Netherlands may reflect the relatively strong competitive performance of these countries within the Single Market — and indeed may contribute to strong performance by funding higher expenditure on education and training and on infrastructure.

So long as major differences in competitive performance remain, it may be possible to sustain considerable differences in tax rates at the national level. The marked differences within Member States in regional and local situations, however, make the national averages highly misleading, and give rise to the question of how far high tax rates and social contributions in areas of high unemployment are a major impediment to job creation where it is most needed.

The regional perspective implies a need for more variation in effective burdens of taxation at local level and, possibly, greater harmonisation of national regimes, with national and Community transfer mechanisms to supplement resources for infrastructure and public services in low-income regions.

CHAPTER 10

Structural Policies and Economic Growth

Long-term funding for public programmes needs to be accompanied by specific measures to recycle present high levels of private savings into investment, especially in Objective 1 and Objective 2 regions, where the need for job creation and the strengthening of economic performance is most acute. The effective use of such funds for the development, or redevelopment, of these regions requires partnership between the public authorities involved, local communities and business and international companies, which are a key source of technical and organisational expertise as well as finance.

During the past decade there has been an increasing accumulation of personal wealth in the form of pension funds and financial investments. The desire for personal financial wealth reflects higher incomes and declining confidence in public institutions. Since 1980, real rates of interest have been higher than in previous decades, offering a good return to private savers, while at the same time raising the cost of funding the public sector.

Accumulation of personal financial wealth needs to be matched by investment in profitable assets, in order to ensure the long-term security of financial funds and to sustain economic growth in line with savings. Low economic growth in the Community, since the mid-1970s, has reflected a failure to convert high savings into profitable investment. Instead, savings have been invested in growing public debt funded at high cost. As the public sector has become impoverished, it has become increasingly difficult to finance investments in infrastructure, environmental improvement, communal services and education, which would be needed to provide the basis for more dynamic economic growth in backward and deindustrialised regions.

Given the reluctance of national governments to allow interference in monetary and fiscal policy, the Community's role in economic management has rightly focused on use of Structural Funds to assist investment in backward regions. But further development of structural policies is, to a large extent, frustrated by institutional factors — by struggles between Member States over the allocation of funds, by questions of control over their deployment, by doubts about the competence, and, in some cases, integrity, of local administrators — as well as by lack of finance.

Without a new investment dynamic, it is hard to foresee an improved rate of economic growth and job creation in backward areas within the Community, or in surrounding regions of Central and Eastern Europe, the Middle East and Africa, which are closely linked to the European economy.

The strongest political base for more dynamic structural policies is not the Community or national level but the local or city level. Specific needs and opportunities are strongly felt by local communities, and the conciliation of business and social interests has to take place mainly at this level. A new dynamic to structural policies might, therefore, be given by a recognition of the primary role of cities and local institutions as the critical agents for development of backward and deindustrialised regions within the Single Market framework.

A second requirement for a strengthening of structural policies is a larger supply of funds. Institutions for finance of structural investment exist, both at Community level (the European Investment Bank) and in many Member States. But the prevailing high level of real interest rates remains a major problem. It is very difficult to justify long-term structural investments if they are required to generate real returns of 6 or 8% per year.

The widespread reliance of Community citizens on positive returns to their financial wealth, which is by now deeply institutionalised, makes a return to zero or negative real interest rates, experienced in the 1960s, very unlikely. At the same time, the accumulation of financial wealth can be expected to continue until the postwar generations begin to reach retirement age in the period after 2005.

During the intervening period, stronger incentives may be required to ensure that accumulating personal financial wealth is invested in infrastructure and business development.

The Edinburgh summit has confirmed that there is little support, at present, for large-scale borrowing by Community institutions to fund the Community's own operations, or to finance transfers within or outside the Community's borders. The alternative is to provide increased stimulus for investment by local institutions, both public and private, especially in backward and deindustrialised regions, where the existing economic base is least adequate.

Subsidies to investment in infrastructure, environmental improvement, education and training can readily be justified in terms of 'externalities' — ie non-revenue benefits to local areas and to the Community as a whole. Because of externalities, the direct returns to the organisation carrying out the investment will not necessarily cover the cost and, therefore, market forces, if left to themselves, will not ensure that such investment takes place. Public sector intervention is, therefore, required to correct the divergence between the private and social rate of return and, in the case of backward regions, in particular, to create the preconditions for attracting private investment on any significant scale.

For example, a 5% interest subsidy extended over the first 10 years of long-term investments would greatly reduce the risk and improve the viability of projects. The cost of subsidising new investments equal to 1% of Community GNP on these terms, building up to a subsidised capital equal to 10% of Community GNP after 10 years — an amount which could make a significant impact in problem regions — would be about 0.5% of Community GNP — approximately the present size of expenditure on structural programmes.

At the present time there is a minor degree of integration between operations of the Community's Structural Funds and lending by the European Investment Bank. A more closely coordinated and more determined effort to promote investment is now badly needed. At the same time, much more scope should be given to private and public institutions at local level to act autonomously in carrying out investment programmes, in place of the present system of complex 'partnerships' largely between public bodies that tend to be dominated in many Member States by Community institutions and national administrations.

CHAPTER 11

Employment Creation Programmes

In parallel with structural investment in regions, where the pace of economic development has to be accelerated, there is a need to establish a framework of legislation to promote job creation through encouragement of small businesses and employment-intensive services. Even if GDP growth in the range 3-4% can be achieved over the rest of the decade, this in itself is unlikely to create enough jobs to bring down unemployment to acceptable levels and, at the same time, provide work for the substantial numbers of women forced up to now to be inactive.

Moreover, outside of backward areas, where the need for economic growth and large-scale investment is acute, growth of production *per se* is in any event less of a priority. In many of the more prosperous parts of the Community, the challenge is to find alternative means of employment creation other than high growth rates. This means accepting the need to manage market forces so as to direct resources into activities which are consistent with the desires of people living in these areas for improvements in the quality of life and, at the same time, to ensure that this is not at the expense of job opportunities.

There is no shortage of activities that can potentially provide jobs while helping to achieve a range of social and environmental objectives. For example, the environmental industry in the Community, which in many areas is still in its infancy, is estimated already to employ over 500,000 people. It offers significant scope for expansion if finance were channelled into reducing pollution, waste management, water treatment, recycling and cleaning up both the natural and urban environment, and if the development of new production processes and new products in this area was encouraged.

Programmes to save energy and to develop new sources and to provide improved education, health, recreation and cultural facilities could together create considerably more jobs.

At the same time, there is a need to encourage the development and growth of small and medium-sized enterprises. This is not only important for the job opportunities that are directly created — often in a more satisfying working environment than large companies are able to provide — but, equally, for the longer-term competitiveness of the Community economy. In many sectors, small businesses provide the research and innovations to feed larger companies, which need continuously to improve their productive efficiency and introduce new products in order to be able to compete on world markets, but which lack the flexibility and individual motivation required to develop new ideas in many areas.

Moreover, because they are local in scale, small and medium-sized businesses are better able to respond to local labour market conditions and demands, including developing and exploring more flexible working arrangements — which might enable, for example, a given volume of work to be shared among increased numbers of people. In the Single Market, and in an increasingly unified financial market, however, small businesses will lose privileged access to local sources of funding, and are likely to find it more difficult to develop.

An effective employment creation programme, combining support for small business and the development of locally-based services, requires the establishment of a Community-level framework that leaves as much discretion as possible over the choice of local actions, but which, at the same time, defines the policy instruments that can be used, and the rules governing their implementation.

The fiscal system, in the form of indirect taxes, tax concessions, exemptions and allowances, as well as public expenditure on grants and subsidies, is the primary means of implementing structural policies in market economies. But given the mobility of business within the unified Community market, it is difficult for national, regional and local governments to use fiscal instruments for structural purposes in the absence of a framework defined at the Community level.

A good example is taxation designed to reduce environmental pollution and to increase the efficiency of use of limited natural resources. Although reduction of pollution and economising on scare resources is of general benefit both to the country taking action and to others, if pollution or resource taxes are introduced unilaterally in any one Member State, that Member State faces the risk of losing business to others that are less careful.

Similar arguments apply to tax incentives that favour small and medium-scale enterprises, or taxes to fund improvements in education, health and social services, and so on. The increased tax burden on larger enterprises again carries the risk that business will be displaced to other parts of the Community where tax rates are lower.

Analogous arguments apply to the enforcement of minimum standards of health and safety and of working conditions as proposed in the Social Charter. Unless these are applied across the whole of the Community, businesses may tend to shift to areas where the authorities are most lax. Indeed, in the absence of an adequate mechanism for transferring income to problem regions to provide a significant incentive for business development, the responsible authorities may be tempted to use lax standards as a substitute means of attracting inward investment. The danger then is that, under pressure of competition, standards throughout the Community will gradually be reduced, and the hard-won advances in working and social conditions will be lost.

CHAPTER 12

Key Issues

The major issues arising from the above analysis that are central to a left strategy for recovery and employment creation, and which, therefore, have to be the focus both of debate and political action, are as follows:

— how to establish sufficient democratic control and accountability of decision-making at the Community level to provide the basis for the coordination of economic policy that is essential for the effective pursuit of adequate rates of economic growth and employment creation in Europe, as well as for supporting development in neighbouring countries in Central and Eastern Europe, North Africa and the Middle East;

— how to rectify the defects in the ERM, demonstrated by the events of the past few months, and establish an operational system with sufficient cooperation between central banks to provide financial stability with the flexibility required to allow for differences in economic conditions and performance between Member States;

— how to establish a framework for the conduct of fiscal policy across the Community that ensures support for governments whose borrowing needs are increased as a result of downturns in economic activity, which avoids them being forced to cut public expenditure and/or raise taxes in recession and which, at the same time, helps them achieve longer-term budgetary goals without unacceptable reductions in spending that weaken their economic and social infrastructure;

— how to strengthen structural policy and ensure that there is a more direct and effective relationship between those responsible for managing both the structural funds and EIB investment at the Community level and the key players at the regional, city or local level, including private business — both large and small — as well as public authorities, who need to act in close partnership to provide an effective force for local economic development;

— how to establish a Community-level framework of fiscal instruments and other discriminatory measures to support small business and local employment creation and to exploit the potential job opportunities provided by the development of environmental and social activities, without damaging the international competitiveness of Community producers.

Summary

1. The European Community is now entering its third decade of slow growth and increased unemployment, accompanied by worsening social conditions in formerly prosperous areas and the steady erosion of standards of social justice that have their roots in Western Europe's social democratic tradition.

As the credibility of programmes for economic growth and social justice diminishes, so political support for left parties has ebbed away in favour of right-wing movements that legitimise individualistic and anarchic solutions to social problems.

2. Further development of the European Community is an absolute necessity for the European left. Without stronger Community policies there is no possibility of implementing a coherent programme to re-establish more dynamic growth and provide a viable context for sustained job creation and more cohesive social policies.

The Community now seems to have reached an historical impasse. Maastricht provides a basis for developing the Community in the required direction. But, so far, preoccupation with securing ratification has diverted attention away from how the Treaty proposals can be translated into a practical framework for policy-making to deliver the objectives of more balanced economic development emphasised in the document.

Governments of Member States, themselves in crisis, increasingly seek to maintain credibility with national electorates by insisting on their primary position as representatives of national interest in the determination of

Community policy, implicitly rejecting wider representation of regional and common European interests.

National electorates, in turn, are suspicious of a Community where policy is determined by horse-trading between governments of twelve independent Member States.

It is difficult for left parties to base their programmes on advocacy of a stronger Community when the Community lacks credibility with electorates.

3. The interruption of economic growth in the Community, at first widely seen as a temporary setback caused by the 1973 and 1979 oil 'shocks', must now be recognised as a more permanent phenomenon.

Two decades of low growth have locked in a vicious circle of fiscal crisis eroding the power of governments to take positive action, and of long-term damage to 'Objective 1' regions whose economic development has been blocked and to 'Objective 2' regions where the closure of traditional industries has not been matched by development of new activities.

4. Inadequate economic growth is reflected in huge regional differences in unemployment and availability of resources for future development. Regional problems which cross both national boundaries and social classes have long-run and deep-seated historical causes and cannot be rectified simply by acceptance of market realities, as maintained by many on the right.

5. A more dynamic growth context is an essential condition for a narrowing in regional disparities. As history shows, the level of unemployment and rate of job creation in Objective 2 regions is extremely sensitive to the rate of economic growth in the Community as a whole, while Objective 1 regions need growth to provide space for more rapid development of competitive export industries and to create jobs for young people and women who, in former times, would either have worked in agriculture or in the home.

In the longer term, stagnation of problem regions within the Community, and the parallel stagnation of similar regions neighbouring its borders to the East and South, deprive the

Community of a growth dynamic. They badly affect the exports of more prosperous areas, increase pressure for immigration, and undermine national fiscal systems.

6. Regional disparities profoundly condition politics at the national and European level. The more prosperous regions have become preoccupied with the need to protect their own position and are reluctant to pay for resource transfers to backward and depressed regions.

National governments do not provide a sufficient channel for the representation of regional interests in the determination of Community policy. Although the preponderance of Objective 1 regions in Greece, Spain, Portugal and Ireland makes the national governments of these countries into a significant lobby, Objective 1 regions elsewhere, and deindustrialised regions in nearly all Member States, are represented, if at all, by national governments whose political base lies mainly in the more prosperous areas.

7. The left's response to slow growth and rising unemployment must combine an assertion of the importance of regional, local and city-level government, which has the immediate task of trying to deal with problems, with parallel emphasis on the need for effective representation at the European level, as the basis for policies necessary to secure more dynamic economic growth in Western Europe and surrounding regions.

The left's programme for further development of the Community should therefore consist, on the one hand, of a demand for stronger and more representative Community institutions, capable of managing economic policy and providing a fully-coordinated monetary framework and, on the other, of increased stress on resource transfers to support local investment and development at the regional or city level.

The overall aim should be a rate of economic growth in the range 3 to 4%, rather than the average rate of little more than 2% achieved over the past two decades, with a concentration of investment and growth of production and employment in Objective 1 and Objective 2 regions, and in similar areas outside the Community's borders.

8. After the experiences of the past few years, monetary stability assumes critical importance as a foundation for sustained investment and expansion of private and public spending. The outcome of the present system of cooperation between central banks inside or outside the ERM has been profoundly damaging, combining high real interest rates with uncertainty about both nominal and real exchange rates.

The existing monetary system has a strong anti-growth bias as central banks, in their preoccupation with avoiding inflation, seek to maintain strong national currencies in competition with one another. Although the Maastricht Treaty provides a framework for eventual consolidation of the monetary system, the details of its proposals, as they have been interpreted by the key players, can now be seen to be seriously inadequate. There is an urgent need to press for an interpretation of the Maastricht proposals emphasising the opportunity they provide, in Stage 2, for much closer cooperation between central banks in the operation of policy.

It is essential that central banks should determine monetary policy on the basis of common European, rather than national, interests, and that monetary policy should be supportive, rather than restrictive, with respect to public and private deficits induced by recession. The function of the monetary system in a context of low growth and high unemployment should be to facilitate investment in infrastructure, improved social services and new business development; not to curb expenditure and bankrupt institutions already damaged by cuts in income.

9. The anti-growth bias of monetary policy has been compounded by an anti-growth bias in attitudes to public spending. Public deficits have been universally regarded as harmful, despite the fact that in many cases they have been caused by downturns in private income and loss of confidence in private assets. Public debt has been forced up, to a large extent, by personal saving not being matched by sufficient business investment. In other words, so far from private investment being 'crowded out' by government borrowing, public debt has been 'crowded in' by a lack of confidence in private investment.

10. The bias against public debt, together with the weakness of national currencies within the EMS, has prevented governments from sustaining spending in recession, contributing to the long-term stagnation of economic growth, and depriving less-prosperous regions of the cheap long-term sources of funds which would be required to start a new cycle of economic growth.

If economic and monetary union is to provide the basis for faster economic growth it is essential that the union should have a sound system for public finance, encouraging stable long-term management of taxation and public spending, and protecting national, regional and local governments against deficits induced by recession.

11. Long-term funding for public programmes needs to be accompanied by specific measures to recycle high private savings into sustained investment, especially in Objective 1 and Objective 2 regions. The redevelopment of these regions needs to be conceived in terms of partnership between city governments, local communities, local businesses and international companies, replacing the bureaucratic concept of partnership between Community, national and local officials on which existing structural programmes are based.

12. In parallel with structural investment, the Community needs a framework of legislation to promote job creation through encouragement of small businesses and employment-intensive services, such as those aimed at improving the environment or at meeting a range of social needs. Such discriminatory action, though at present contrary to the Single Market philosophy, need not damage the competitiveness of Community producers since it would be directed at businesses and activities not involved in international trade. Indeed, over the long-term, by encouraging the development of new ideas, it could strengthen competitiveness.

If the large business sector continues to dominate the small, and if a substantial proportion of the population remains unemployed or inactive, the foundations for future prosperity are likely to be progressively eroded. Regions become heavily dependent on the ebb and flow of investment provided by international business and, therefore, remain at the mercy of developments over which they have little or no control.

Unless small-scale, locally-based activities are legitimised and given some degree of financial privilege, it is impossible to see how contemporary demands for universal and flexible participation in the labour market can be accommodated. In the longer term, the small business sector provides the fund of experience, new ideas and innovation that facilitates development of large businesses competing on a global scale.

13. The key task now and in the future is to translate the need for policy action at the Community and local level into a concrete programme of action, defining not only the form and scale of measures that should be included, but, no less importantly, the parallel changes in political institutions and policy-making procedures that are essential if there is to be effective democratic control over decision-making.

THE EUROPEAN RECOVERY PROGRAMME

Restoring Full Employment

Ken Coates MEP & Michael Barratt Brown (editors)

Dismal though the present outlook for employment in Europe appears, there is a way forward, out of crisis. That way depends upon joint action. In the circumstances of the 1990s, such joint action should naturally be led by the European Commission, and co-ordinated with member governments. Elsewhere in the world, Japan, and, on a smaller scale, the United States, have already initiated their own plans to put people back to work.

Of course, the more thorough the convergence of incomes and social cohesion can be throughout the European Community, the more dynamic the recovery will prove. Shorter working time also has a key role to play. But all this will require completely different policies from the restrictions on public expenditure that obsess so many governments in Europe, and above all from the dogmas that still dominate the reflexes of government in Britain.

CONTENTS include: The European Recovery Programme (Ken Coates MEP); Funding and Planning Recovery (Stuart Holland); Economic and Monetary Union and the European Community Budget (Sir Donald MacDougall); Where We Are (Jacques Delors); Maastricht and All That (Wynne Godley); Money, Debt & Slump (Michael Barratt Brown); The Social Dimension (John Hughes, Peter Townsend); Trade Unions' Role (Rodney Bickerstaffe, Roger Lyons)

ISBN 0 85124 539 0
cloth £30.00

ISBN 0 85124 549 8
paper £8.95

200 pages

Elf Books 7

The SOCIAL CHARTER *and the* SINGLE EUROPEAN MARKET

John Hughes

We can hardly understate the importance for the future political economy of Europe of the wide-ranging developments and changes being set in motion in the course of constructing a single market for the European Community. At the same time, the debate about the Social Charter and the Action Programme embodies two interlinked dimensions of social and political concern following from this development. In this luminous text, John Hughes shows how the new needs of equity require a rapid evolution of new norms of social and political practice.

Addressing social partners such as trade unionists and consumers' groups, he argues that the Community's emphasis on social dialogue and the equitable extension of social rights need to go hand in hand with large-scale programmes of expenditure to help disadvantaged reqions, to combat discrimination against part-time workers, reflected so starkly in women's inferior pay for work of equal value, to tackle long-term unemployment, and to meet the needs of young people entering the labour market. In this way, and with persistent effort, we can constitute the social dimension of the single European market.

Hugh McMahon MEP contributes a checklist on how the Social Charter is faring from the viewpoints of the Commission's Action Programme and that of the European Parliament.

John Hughes is consultant to the Trade Union Research Unit (TURU), Ruskin College, Oxford.

ISBN 085124 524 2 £6.95 paper
ISBN 085124 523 4 £20.00 cloth

Elf Books 1

SPOKESMAN
for European Labour Forum

Printed in Dunstable, United Kingdom

91342767R00042